KU-706-595

Archaeology

Discovering the past

John Orna-Ornstein

THE BRITISH MUSEUM PRESS

© 2002 The Trustees of The British Museum

John Orna-Ornstein has asserted his moral right to be identified as the author of this work.

First published in 2002 by The British Museum Press
A division of The British Museum Company Ltd
46 Bloomsbury Street, London WC1B 3QQ

ISBN 0 7141 3006 0

A catalogue record for this title is available from the British Library.

Designed and typeset in Stone by Fiona Webb
Cover design by Slatter-Anderson
Printed and bound in Belgium by Proost NV

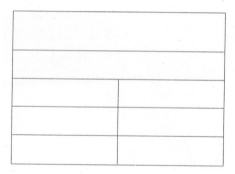

For Emily and Benjamin

Illustration acknowledgements

Photographs are © The British Museum, taken by The British Museum Photography and Imaging Department, unless otherwise stated.

The illustrations on pages 11, 19, 20, 21 and 26 were drawn by Victor Ambrus.
The digital artwork on p. 17 was created by Mark Timson/New Media Unit/The British Museum.
The map on p. 35 was drawn by ML Design.

Lesley and Roy Adkins Picture Library: p. 8 top; p. 15 left; p. 16 bottom; p. 27 top left; p. 39 top.
The Ancient Art and Architecture Collection Ltd/R. Sheridan: p. 36 bottom.
Aspect Picture Library Ltd: p. 24 top.
Mike Baillie: p. 21 top right.
Stephen Benson: p. 9 top left.
Mensun Bound: p. 18 top.
The Bridgeman Art Library: p. 6 centre (*Charles Towneley and his Friends in the Towneley Gallery, 33 Park St, Westminster, 1781–3*, oil on canvas, by Johann Zoffany (1733–1810), Towneley Hall Art Gallery and Museum, Burnley, Lancashire/ Bridgeman Art Library).
Caroline Cartwright, Dept of Scientific Research, The British Museum: p. 31 bottom.
Collections: p. 5 top; p. 10 centre; p. 33 bottom.
Crown copyright. NMR (15406/20): p. 13 centre.
James P. Delgado: p. 18 bottom.
Dr Clark L. Erickson: p. 5 bottom.
Joyce Filer: p. 27 top right and centre; p. 28 right and left; p. 30 centre.
Werner Forman: p. 38 top left.
John Frost Newspapers: p. 8 bottom.
Professor Norman Hammond: p. 24 bottom; p. 25 bottom left and right.
John W. Lord: p. 32 bottom.
Nigel Macbeth: p. 26 centre.
© Mary Rose Trust: p. 19 top.
Dr Sam Moorhead: p. 14; p. 15 centre right and bottom; p. 30 right.
Peter Newark's American Pictures: p. 6 bottom.
Pepys Library, Magdalene College, Cambridge: p. 19 centre left.
Paul Pettitt: p. 36 centre.
Pitt Rivers Museum, University of Oxford: p. 17 bottom right.
Réunion des Musées Nationaux/R.G. Ojeda; Portrait of Champollion by Cogniet Léon (1794–1880): p. 37 bottom left.
Royal National Throat, Nose and Ear Hospital: p. 30 left.
© Salisbury and South Wiltshire Museum: p. 7 centre and bottom.
Science Photo Library: p. 21 bottom left.
Spinks: p. 19 centre right.
Stratascan Ltd: p. 13 bottom left.
Helen Tayler: p. 4 bottom left.
Vancouver Maritime Museum: p. 18 centre.
Peter Waddell, Parks Canada: p. 19 bottom left.
© Elaine A. Wakefield/Wessex Archaeology: p. 13 top and bottom right.

Leabharlann Chontae na Mí	
Meath County Library	
0195361	-
L B C	977009
930.1	E15.48
-3 SEP 2002	~/06/2002

WITHDRAWN FROM STOCK

Contents

Introduction

Archaeology is the study of people who lived in the past from the objects they have left behind. Sometimes these objects are spectacular – perhaps pieces of jewellery or beautiful sculptures. More often, they are the remains of everyday life, such as pieces of pottery or coins that have been thrown away or lost. By studying these objects it is possible to learn the stories of people who lived thousands of years ago, often long before any history was written down to tell us about them.

What does an archaeologist do?

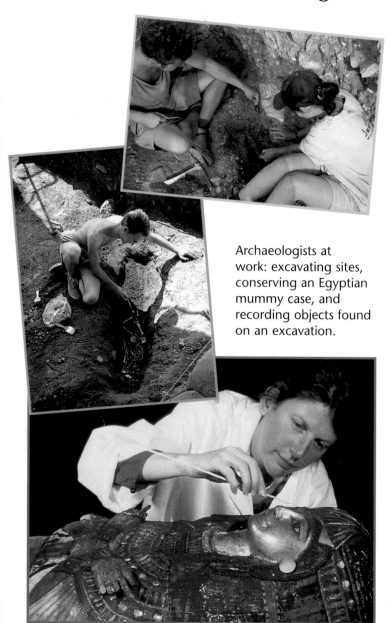

Archaeologists at work: excavating sites, conserving an Egyptian mummy case, and recording objects found on an excavation.

Archaeologists excavate, or uncover, traces of people who lived in the past. The places where these traces are found are called 'sites'. You might find archaeologists working on a sandy site in the deserts of Egypt, diving to search the remains of a shipwreck, or excavating a medieval cemetery in the middle of a busy city.

Archaeology is not only about finding things. It is also about understanding the things that are found. So you might also see archaeologists in a laboratory staring at tiny remains through a microscope or in a library studying reports of excavations in the past. From the remains of the past, archaeologists try to understand what people were like and why they acted as they did.

Why is the past often underground?

Discoveries are often made by digging in the places where people used to live. As old buildings are destroyed or fall into ruin, layers of soil or rubbish pile over them or new buildings are built on top. The ground level gradually rises as the centuries go by, so burying the remains of the past.

A nineteenth-century building gradually falls into ruin.

The context of this 6,000 year old pot is the grave in which it was found.

Context

Bones or pieces of pottery, for example, can tell us something about the past, but they tell us a lot more when they are found with other objects in the place where they were left all those years ago. The surroundings of an object – where it comes from and how it relates to other objects – is called its 'context'. The context of an object helps archaeologists to understand its background: how old it is, who used it, and how it was used.

Does the past matter?

One reason for finding out about the past is so that we can learn about things that are important in the present. An example of this is in Peru, in South America, where archaeologists are helping local people to farm their land more successfully by showing them how the Incas did it hundreds of years ago. But there is another, less practical reason for learning about the past. We all know how important our memories are, and how empty our lives would be if we had no memory. Archaeologists provide the memory not of individuals but of whole tribes, races, regions and countries. We can often learn useful lessons from the past.

In the community of Huatta in Peru, raised fields in the ancient Inca style have been reconstructed. These fields are planted with potatoes.

Searchers

Throughout history people have collected ancient objects for their beauty or for their value. In the 6th century BC Nabonidus was king of Babylon (in modern-day Iraq). He excavated the temple of Shamath at Sippar to try to find out who built it, and discovered remains from more than 2,000 years earlier. An interest in the past ran in the king's family, for his daughter started the world's first museum of ancient objects in the city of Ur. From the 15th century AD onwards it became normal for wealthy people to have collections of 'curiosities' ranging from fossils to ancient coins.

A stone monument of Nabonidus, king of Babylon from 555 to 539 BC.

◀ The magnificent sculpture collection of Charles Townley (1737-1805). This private museum was in his dining room! After Charles Townley's death, his Roman and Greek sculptures went to The British Museum in London.

The birth of archaeology

Many archaeological excavations took place during the second half of the 18th century and the first half of the 19th century. Most, however, were unscientific and poorly recorded. But gradually a growing number of excavators began to realize the importance of recording everything that was found, rather than just recovering treasure.

 **THOMAS JEFFERSON (1743–1826)**

Thomas Jefferson is best known for being the third president of the United States of America. Archaeologists, however, remember him for carrying out one of the first scientific excavations in the history of archaeology. In 1784 Jefferson dug a trench across a burial mound on his property in Virginia. He carefully recorded everything he found. The future president was then able to suggest that the mound had been built by ancestors of the Native Americans living there at the time.

A framework for the past

In the 19th century archaeologists divided prehistory into the 'Stone Age', 'Bronze Age' and 'Iron Age' according to the tools that people used. These names are still in use today. At about the same time a fierce debate was raging about the age of mankind. The Bible seemed to suggest that the world was created about 6,000 years ago, but a number of discoveries proved that the world was much, much older. One of the most important discoveries was the excavation of tools in the Somme Valley of France, which were made from the bones of long-extinct animals.

Modern archaeology

Some of the excavation methods we use today originated in the late 19th century in the work of archaeologists such as Augustus Pitt-Rivers (see pages 16–17).

In 1696 this handaxe was found in London close to the bones of an elephant or mammoth. We now know that the handaxe is about 350,000 years old and was made at a time when elephants still lived in Britain.

The excavation of Wor Barrow at Cranborne Chase, the property of Augustus Pitt-Rivers. His excavations set new standards.

In the second half of the 20th century archaeologists began to realize that their aim should be to explain what happened in the past, and not just describe it. Why, for example, did people begin to use tools, and why did they start to live in villages? Explaining as well as describing change remains the main aim of archaeology in the 21st century.

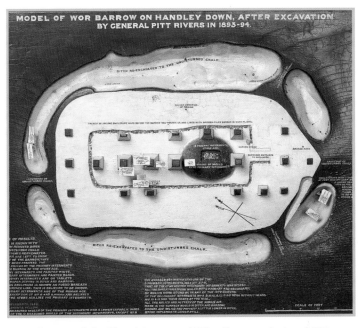

Wooden models, like this one of Wor Barrow, helped Pitt-Rivers to record his excavations.

Famous excavations

A handful of early archaeological excavations were so important and exciting that they attracted attention throughout the world. Discoveries like the tomb of Tutankhamun, the cities of Troy and Pompeii and the graves of Ur have inspired generations of archaeologists and the general public alike.

A street in Pompeii with the pavements and buildings clearly visible.

Pompeii and Herculaneum

Some of the first large scientific excavations were of the ancient cities of Pompeii and Herculaneum in southern Italy. These two Roman cities had been buried under ash and lava when the volcano Vesuvius erupted in AD 79. Early excavations took place in the 18th century, but it was not until the 19th century that careful, well-recorded archaeology began to reveal Pompeii and Herculaneum looking much as they had nearly 2,000 years ago.

Tutankhamun

The discovery of Tutankhamun's tomb, as shown in an early 20th century illustrated newspaper.

One archaeological discovery grabbed the world's attention more than any other. In 1922 an Englishman called Howard Carter discovered the tomb of the Egyptian pharaoh Tutankhamun. Inside the tomb was the mummified pharaoh in a wonderfully carved gold coffin, together with dozens of beautiful and valuable objects.

Tutankhamun had ruled for only nine years, between 1361 and 1351 BC, but he was buried with one of the greatest treasures ever discovered by archaeologists.

This Egyptian statue, dating to about 1320 BC, has the face of the boy-king Tutankhamun.

The Incas

In the second half of the 19th century, some archaeologists became fascinated with the Incas, a civilization that built a huge empire in South America during the 15th and 16th centuries. One of the

Intricate stone carving from the Inca city of Pachacamac.

most important sites to be excavated during this period was Pachacamac, on the central coast of Peru. A German, Max Uhle, was able to identify the site as an important religious centre and today Uhle is seen as the founder of Peruvian archaeology.

An-yang

An-yang was the capital of the Shang dynasty that ruled China between about 1766 and 1122 BC. The city was rediscovered in the early 20th century and, from 1928, excavations were carried out by the Chinese archaeologist Li Chi. He carefully uncovered more than 300 tombs, including important royal burial sites.

A range of wonderful objects – including beautiful bronze containers, decorated chariots and jade weapons and ornaments – show how advanced the Shang dynasty was.

Bronze ritual vessel of the Shang dynasty, decorated with two rams' heads.

Palaces of Assyria and graves of Ur

The Assyrian empire, based in what is now Iraq, reached its height in the 7th century BC. Until the mid-19th century the cities and palaces of Assyria had long been forgotten. In the 1840s archaeologists began to uncover the remains of magnificent

This 4,500 year old lyre was found at Ur.

temples and palaces. Later, in the same country, a British archaeologist named Sir Leonard Woolley found at the royal city of Ur the graves of a people called the Sumerians. Inside were hundreds of records cut on stone or clay tablets, as well as magnificent treasures.

A huge winged bull from the ancient Assyrian city of Nimrud (right) and a picture of its discovery in the nineteenth century.

DISCOVERY OF THE GIGANTIC HEAD.

What is left?

Most objects are destroyed or eventually decay after they stop being used. Nevertheless, it is amazing how much of the past survives. Sometimes, even delicate items can be preserved for hundreds or thousands of years if the conditions they are buried in are right. The difficult job for an archaeologists is to piece together the past from the remains that are left. Most of these remains are just the rubbish of earlier civilizations. Some objects were deliberately buried, but many others were simply thrown away or lost.

A young bull from ancient Egypt, deliberately preserved by mummification.

Pottery is very durable. This ancient Greek pot has survived unbroken for about 2,500 years.

A modern rubbish dump. What do you think future archaeologists might discover about us from the rubbish we throw away?

A load of rubbish

Archaeologists mostly deal with the rubbish of people who are long dead. This can range from broken pots to discarded animal bones. A good way to think about what archaeologists uncover is to look at the contents of your own rubbish bin. What sort of things do you throw away? Which of them are likely to survive if your rubbish was buried for a hundred years? Then try to imagine what an archaeologist would discover about you from this type of evidence.

Preservation

Some objects, such as pieces of pottery, can survive for thousands of years in most conditions. Others usually survive only if they have been burned or end up in peat bogs, lakes, deserts or frozen in ice. These are all examples of environments that help to preserve organic objects.

This Egyptian man died more than 5,000 years ago. His body has been preserved by the dry conditions of a shallow desert grave.

Wet and dry, hot and cold

Decay takes place most rapidly where there is a combination of water and oxygen. Some of the most spectacular remains of the past have been found in deserts, where the lack of water slows down decay. In such conditions, human bodies, food and cloth sometimes survive. Other extraordinary remains have been recovered from cold areas, such as Alaska and the Alps. At Pazyryk, in Siberia, archaeologists uncovered a number of richly furnished burials dating back to 400 BC. The burials included well-preserved bodies and objects made of cloth, wood, fur and leather.

Lack of oxygen means that organic remains can also be preserved in very wet conditions – peat bogs and fens, for example. At an incredible 6,000 years of age, the Sweet Track is the oldest wooden pathway that has ever been discovered.

The Sweet Track, a raised wooden walkway, preserved for thousands of years by the bog it was built to cross.

In focus THE VINDOLANDA TABLETS

Roman letters written on thin slices of wood, known as the Vindolanda Tablets, have survived for 2,000 years thanks to the waterlogged conditions they were buried in. The letters were found at the site of the Roman fort of Vindolanda, near Hadrian's Wall in the north of England.

One of the letters is an invitation to a birthday party from a Roman lady called Claudia Severa to her friend Sulpicia Lepidina. Another letter was written to a soldier, perhaps from his mother, saying 'I have sent you [some] pairs of socks ... and two pairs of underpants ...'

Landscapes of the past

Archaeology often begins in a library or public records office. Although one of the most important tasks for archaeologists is to find and record sites and features, they also use a variety of methods to study whole landscapes at a time. So rather than just looking at a single site, they look for all sorts of clues to help them find traces of past human activity over a wide area. Old maps, records and place names are often good places to start. Some evidence that is invisible from the ground can be seen clearly from the air. And special machines can often find walls and other features, even when they are buried underground.

Maps and place names

Most archaeology begins with a careful study of documents. Maps – both old and new – may provide valuable information. Old buildings or earthworks are often marked, and sometimes it is possible to detect old settlements from the shape of fields or streets on a map. In other cases, names recorded on a map give a hint of what may once have stood there.

In southwest Europe, for example, many stone tombs have been found from place names that mean 'stone' or 'tomb'. In England, it is possible to identify Viking Age sites from places names, which often end in -by or -thorpe. Examples are Whitby in Yorkshire and Scunthorpe in north Lincolnshire.

An Englishman called John Speed drew detailed maps of Britain in the late 16th and early 17th centuries. They provide a wealth of information for modern historians and archaeologists.

Field walking

Traces of ancient human activity can often be seen if you look closely at the ground. Small objects, such as shards of pottery, coins or pieces of building material, may be clues that a building is buried underground. Field walking involves the careful collection and mapping of all these small objects.

▶ Field walking to gather and record finds often provides the first evidence of a new site.

An aerial photograph of the Iron Age hill fort at Yarnbury, Wiltshire. The remains of an earlier structure show up inside the main ramparts.

Aerial photography

The remains of human activity can sometimes be seen from the air, even when they are buried underground. In dry weather crops may grow poorly on thin soil lying over buried buildings and roads. Or crops may grow unusually well in the deep soil that is the result of long-forgotten pits and ditches being filled in over the years. Either of these effects can reveal signs of ancient settlements when they are photographed from the air.

Looking more closely

Once a site has been discovered, it is important to find out as much about it as possible before any excavation starts. Digging is expensive - and destroys the site that is being investigated! A variety of machines can be used to pick up changes in the soil that show where features are buried. Some machines use radar, others use methods called magnetic variation, echo-sounding and resistivity. Different methods are used to find different sorts of features.

A magnetometer trace which shows the remains of Iron Age roundhouse enclosures. ▶

▲ This magnetometer can detect the tiny magnetic fields produced by walls or other features hidden in the soil.

Excavation

Excavation means making a hole in the ground, and it comes from a Latin word meaning 'to hollow out'. The term is normally used to describe the way archaeologists dig up a site. Surprisingly, excavation is normally a last resort. This is because digging is destructive. Once you have dug up a site it is gone for ever. All that is left is the record the archaeologists made and perhaps some solid remains, such as building foundations. If a site is about to be destroyed by building work or a new road, then excavation is probably essential. Where this is not the case, other methods, such as field walking, may provide all of the information we need to know.

If archaeologists decide that a site must be dug they plan the excavation carefully. Where should they begin? How large an area should be uncovered? These, and many other questions must all be answered before they start. Studying the available information, perhaps in a local library (page 12), and then digging small test trenches may help archaeologists make these decisions.

Tools

All sorts of tools are used to excavate sites. While large mechanical diggers remove soil that does not contain archaeological evidence, the most important tool for much excavation work is a small hand trowel. Spoons or even dental picks may also be needed for uncovering delicate objects. Measuring and drawing equipment and cameras are also vital to help archaeologists record a site properly.

◄ A trowel and small instruments including paintbrushes were used to excavate this delicate skeleton of a child.

▲ A deep section with many layers, covering over 2,000 years of history, at a site in Israel.

◄ A shallow section of a hill-fort excavation.

Digging

Soil is normally laid down gradually over long periods of time (page 5). Once soil has been disturbed – by digging a pit, for example, or by building a wall or even by the burrowing of an animal – the signs will always be seen in the ground.

Excavations at an ancient temple in Thebes (modern Luxor) in Egypt.

One of the most important skills an archaeologist needs is to be able to spot these disturbances, whether they are natural or caused by people. Signs of disturbance might be seen as a change in soil colour or even a change in how the soil feels. Each different area of soil represents a context (page 5), and as each context is removed the archaeologist tries to build up a picture of how it was created. The objects found from each context are important clues in doing this, so each one is labelled and kept separate.

Recording

Every part of a site must be carefully recorded. Some parts are destroyed when they are excavated and the only records of them are those made by the archaeologists. A measured survey of the site is carried out, photographs are taken, record sheets are filled in and detailed scale drawings of all features and deposits are made. Once the exact positions and circumstances of any objects have been noted, they can then be removed from the site for further study.

▲ An archaeologist records every detail of a burial.

▶ At this site at Tell Jezreel, Israel, both photographic towers and a fire engine were used to take aerial photographs.

Reconstructing the past

The task of archaeologists is to build up a picture of what life in the past was like – not for their own benefit, but so that other people might understand it. To help them do this, archaeologists publish details of any sites that are excavated. They also preserve sites so that they can be seen by the public or create computer pictures to show what a building might once have looked like.

A detailed excavation report describing objects found at Soba in Central Sudan.

Publication

Publication is one of the basic duties of an archaeologist. There is little point in excavating a site if nobody else sees the information discovered. So, in a 'site publication' all of the detailed evidence gathered during an excavation is summarized. Archaeologists will then try to explain this evidence by comparing it with evidence from other sites. A site publication is likely to include plans of any buildings or other important features, and it may also include artist's drawings showing how the site may have looked before it was buried.

Preserving and reconstructing

Sometimes the remains of a site are so important and interesting that they are preserved so that the public can see them. The remains may need to be strengthened, or 'consolidated', first to make them safe and then to ensure they last many years into the future. Occasionally, ancient buildings have actually been rebuilt in their original position. This happened with the Minoan palace of Knossos on the Greek island of Crete.

A partial reconstruction of the Minoan palace at Knossos, Crete, built by Sir Arthur Evans in the early 20th century.

The problem with physical reconstruction is that the reconstruction can never be more than a best guess – it may be wrong! A better option is to use computer images to help people imagine a site in the past. 'Virtual reality' allows us to wander around an ancient building or town that disappeared thousands of years ago.

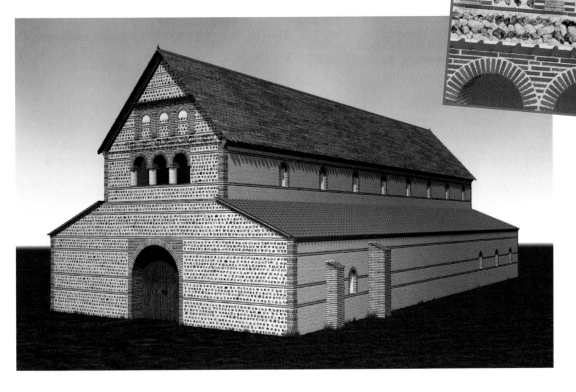

This computer reconstruction of a Roman barn from Lullingstone, England, can be viewed from any angle and includes an enormous amount of detail.

Profile **GENERAL AUGUSTUS PITT-RIVERS (1827–1900)**

General Augustus Pitt-Rivers was a very important figure in archaeology, transforming it from treasure hunting into the scientific process we know today. After retiring from the army, Pitt-Rivers carried out some excavations on his land in Wiltshire, England. He treated his excavations a little like a military campaign. Each site was fully excavated and the location of every object, large or small, was recorded. When he had finished, his work was published in great detail in four volumes. In many ways Pitt-Rivers was years ahead of his time, but unfortunately many archaeologists of his day were slow to follow this inspirational lead.

Pitt-Rivers left one of these tokens in each of his excavations, so that future archaeologists could see that the site had already been disturbed.

Underwater archaeology

In 1853 a particularly dry winter led to unusually low water levels in several of Switzerland's mountain lakes. As water levels dropped a series of extraordinary lakeside villages, normally hidden by the water, began to emerge. The investigation of these neolithic settlements attracted worldwide attention and is often seen as the birth of underwater archaeology. From these early days, underwater excavation has developed into a highly sophisticated process. In the sea, archaeologists investigate shipwrecks, sunken harbours and even drowned cities.

Wrecks and underwater sites

Finding the remains of the past underwater can be a tremendous challenge. Shipwrecks or drowned settlements may be buried under layers of sand

The *Lusitania*. Her wreck was found in deep water off the coast of Ireland with the aid of sonar scanners.

or silt and located tens or hundreds of metres below the surface of the water. Written evidence, which sometimes records exactly where ships are sunk or settlements located, is a useful start in the search. Once archaeologists have an idea of where to look, they can use modern scientific survey methods, such as sonar scanners, to help them. Sonar scanners bounce sound waves off the seabed. Wrecks or other features can be identified because they produce distortions in the sound waves. One of the first wrecks to be discovered using sonar was the *Lusitania*, a cruise ship sunk by a German submarine in the First World War.

Underwater excavation

Underwater excavation is often difficult. Vast amounts of sand may need to be removed, and then structures and objects recorded, just as they would be on land, before being lifted to the surface. Fortunately, many of these tasks have been made easier by new technology. Scuba equipment gives divers freedom of movement; suction hoses remove large quantities of sand in minutes; and miniature submarines permit exploration at great depths.

A submersible preparing to explore the wreck of the *Titanic*, which sank on her maiden voyage in 1912.

The remains of the Tudor warship *Mary Rose*.

When a sunken ship is in good condition it is possible to raise and preserve its remains. The English warship *Mary Rose*, which sank in 1545, was excavated between 1969 and 1982. The ship is now kept in a special dock where it is sprayed with water for at least twenty hours a day.

The *Mary Rose*, shown in a list of King Henry VIII's warships called the Anthony Roll. ▶

Ships and cargoes

More than a hundred sunken vessels have been excavated by archaeologists, and some carried cargoes that make them particularly interesting. The *Madrague de Giens*, a merchant vessel from ancient Rome, contained more than 6,000 *amphorae* (large pottery containers) of wine. The *Kas*, from southern Turkey, dating back to the 14th century BC, had a cargo of twenty enormous copper ingots weighing a total of more than six tonnes.

Occasionally, shipwrecks contain fabulous wealth. This treasure comes from a wreck discovered off the coast of Uruguay in South America. It included more than 1,500 large gold coins and 40 gold ingots and bars. ▶

In focus — THE RED BAY WRECK, CANADA

Underwater archaeology has provided a fascinating picture of whale hunting at Red Bay, Labrador, Canada, in the 16th century. In 1978 archaeologists found a galleon called *San Juan*, which sank in Red Bay harbour in 1565. Archaeologists excavated the site between 1980 and 1984. Their careful work allowed them to reconstruct the ship accurately and to gain an impression of what life must have been like for the sailors who worked on it. Items recovered during the excavation included polar bear bones, showing that the crew hunted animals other than whales.

A diver photographs timbers of the Red Bay Wreck

How old is it?

Many sites were occupied for a long time, and this means that archaeologists sometimes find objects of very different dates all in the same area. One of the first things they must do is decide the age of the things they discover. The shapes, colours and patterns of objects change with time and sometimes these features give important clues about when they were made. Different shapes and patterns were popular at different times, just like fashions today. Looking at changes in the appearance of objects – or 'typology' – was once the main way of dating finds. Typology was mostly used in combination with 'stratigraphy' (see below). A major change came in 1949 with the invention of radiocarbon dating, and other scientific dating techniques have since appeared.

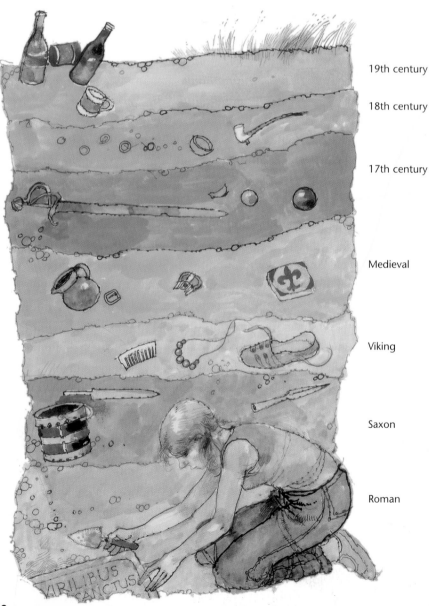

19th century

18th century

17th century

Medieval

Viking

Saxon

Roman

Stratigraphy

An archaeological site is a bit like a layer cake. The top layer is the most recent and the other layers get older as they get deeper. The simplest way to decide the 'chronology' of objects which are the oldest and which the most recent is by seeing in what order they are dug up. The newest things are normally going to be in the layers of soil closest to the surface. The oldest things may be buried deep underground When objects are found in layers according to their age, archaeologists call this 'stratification'.

Uncovering the centuries: Layers near the top are normally the most recent. Those buried deep underground may be thousands of years old.

Radiocarbon dating

A great revolution in archaeology was caused by the discovery in 1949 of carbon dating. All living things contain tiny amounts of radioactive carbon, known as carbon-14. When a plant or animal dies its amount of carbon-14 decreases, or decays. Scientists know exactly how long this takes, and so by examining the amount of carbon-14 that is still left in the remains they can tell how old the item must be. The main limit of radio-carbon dating is that it works only on things that were once alive, such as bone, grain or charcoal, and on things that are less than 50,000 years old. Other scientific dating techniques also rely on radioactive decay, and some of these can go back much further than 50,000 years.

Radiocarbon dating equipment.

The Sweet Track is a prehistoric trackway from Somerset in southern England. Tree ring dating shows that it was built in 3807 or 3806 BC. ▶

Tree rings

Have you ever noticed the rings in a cut piece of wood? The former American president Thomas Jefferson (1743–1826) was one of the first people to suggest the study of these tree rings as a method of dating wooden objects.

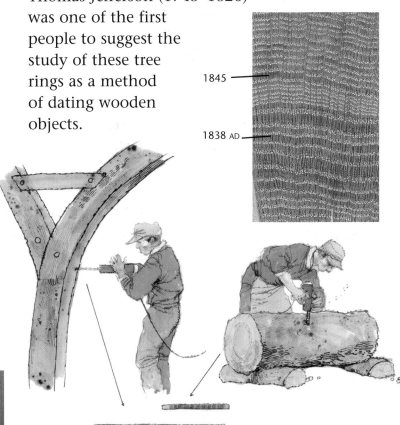

1845
1838 AD

Most trees produce a ring of new wood every year. The thickness of these rings varies according to the climate in any particular year. Archaeologists measure the rings, comparing one tree with another, and in this way build up a long sequence of tree rings representing the past. The rings in pieces of wood discovered on an archaeological site can be compared with this sequence. Sometimes the age of the wood can be determined quite accurately.

Leabharlann
0195361
Contae na Mhí

Conservation

Conservators working on an Iron Age site. They lift fragile objects in blocks of soil held together by bandages, before taking them back to the work-shop for conservation.

The job of an archaeological 'conservator' is to make sure that all of the material recovered from an excavation stays in as good a condition as possible. Objects are normally stable when they are found, but altering their conditions by uncovering them can change all that. Conservators must also supervise the cleaning of objects, either by hand or with chemicals. One of the golden rules of conservation is to use whenever possible treatments that are 'reversible'. This means that if anything goes wrong they can be changed back.

On site

Most conservation work takes place in the laboratory, but essential 'first aid' is often needed at the archaeological site. The first task of a conservator may be to help excavate fragile objects. They are then responsible for making sure that excavated objects are not decaying. Wet objects, for example, are stored in water or in a wet tissues to stop them drying out, while organic material, such as wood or cloth, is usually treated to prevent it going mouldy. Some simple cleaning also takes place on site. Pottery and stone can normally be cleaned in water using a soft-bristled toothbrush.

In the laboratory

More complicated treatments and cleaning take place in the laboratory. Objects must be carefully stabilized so that they do not decay. In the case of wet wood, for example, this could mean replacing the water with special chemicals to prevent it shrinking as it dries out. Objects may also need delicate cleaning to allow them to be studied by archaeologists or other specialists. Fortunately, conservators have a range of modern tools and chemicals to help them examine and treat the huge variety of material that is recovered from excavations.

Painstaking reconstruction of a large pot.

Conservation of an Egyptian mummy portrait.

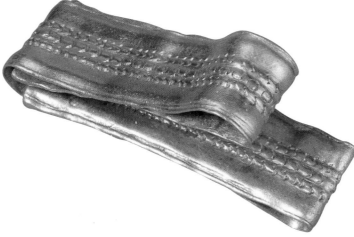

The medieval coin on the left is hard to identify. The coin on the right has been cleaned and can be fully identified.

Restoration?

Conservators don't usually restore objects unless it is essential. Some objects, however, do need to be repaired or restored, particularly if they are to go on display in a museum. Pots are sometimes rebuilt and holes in damaged cloth may be repaired. But any restoration should be visible – at least to the trained eye – and it should also be reversible. The importance of this became apparent with the remains of a helmet recovered from the excavation of an Anglo-Saxon burial mound at Sutton Hoo, England. The helmet was originally reconstructed a decade after its discovery in 1939. However, ideas about what the helmet originally looked like changed over the years, and in 1968 the helmet was taken apart and reconstructed again – but this time it looked quite different!

There was no need for conservators to restore this Roman bracelet to its original shape. The fact that it has been bent provides useful information about the history of the object. Its owner clearly cared more about the value of the gold than about wearing the bracelet as jewellery.

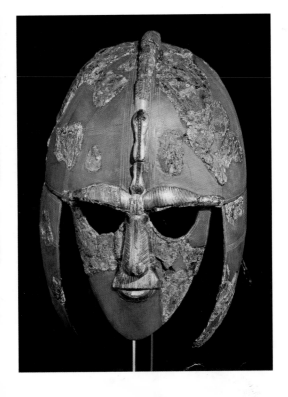

The Anglo-Saxon helmet from Sutton Hoo. Five hundred fragments of the helmet have been carefully reconstructed to give an accurate idea of what it looked like (left). From this evidence the replica (right) could be made.

What was the world like?

In order to understand how people in the past behaved we must first build up a picture of what their world might have been like. When archaeologists investigate a site they try to discover as much as possible about the environment of the time. This includes such factors as the climate, animals and plants that might once have existed there.

Plant remains prove that the Sahara desert was once wooded. Ancient rock paintings show domestic cattle that would be difficult to look after in the Sahara today.

Climate

Climate, or long-term weather, has a huge influence on plant and animal life. Parts of the world that are barren deserts today were once lush grasslands or dense forests. And some areas that are now in temperate regions were, thousands of years ago, part of a frozen landscape. Archaeologists gather information about past climate from a number of sources. One of the most important of these is the plant and animal life itself. Another is the landscape, which has been shaped and moulded by the climate over millions of years.

Plants

Archaeologists are keen to discover the range of plants that people in the past would have encountered. A lot of information comes from studying very tiny plant remains, such as pollen. Pollen can tell us whether an area was once covered in trees or grass, or even if it was a desert, because the types of plant that grow in these different climates all have different types of pollen. Larger plant remains, such as fragments of charred wood or grain, are recovered by sieving the soil dug out from a site. These remains give us proof about which plants were used and eaten by people in the past.

Wet sieving of soil is an effective way to find small, light plant remains.

Animals

Even minor changes in the environment can have a big impact on small animals and insects. The appearance and disappearance of tiny animals therefore provides some of the best information archaeologists have about past changes. Evidence from ancient pollen grains suggests that the number of elm trees in Britain declined about 5,000 years ago. Archaeologists were not sure why this might have happened until they realized that the decline occurred at the same time as the appearance of a tiny beetle called Scolytus scolytus. This beetle is known to be responsible for Dutch elm disease, which still kills elm trees today. The remains of large animals found in an archaeological excavation tell us other things about the past, such as what our ancestors used to eat (pages 30-31).

The remains of water snails tell us that this Late Bronze Age site at Runnymede in southern Britain was once almost an island in the river Thames.

In focus   CUELLO, BELIZE

Archaeologists have built up an accurate picture of the environment and the diet of people at an ancient Mayan site at Cuello in northern Belize. They analysed small plant and animal remains from the soil.
The most important plant food was maize (corn), but careful wet sieving has shown that a variety of root crops such as manioc and sweet potato were also eaten. Both maize and root crops were farmed in fields near Cuello. People hunted wild deer, armadillos and freshwater turtles for meat. It seems they also kept tame dogs, feeding them on scraps - and ate the dogs too. Study of human bones from the site suggests that the men drank beer made from maize.

▲ Plant and animal remains from Cuello, including the bones of deer and armadillo.

◄ The main trench at Cuello, with a small pyramid in the background.

Faces from the past

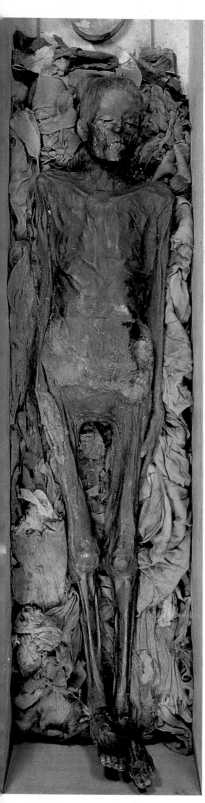

The Ancient Egyptians deliberately preserved their dead by mummifying them. This unwrapped mummy is 2,500 years old.

One of the main aims of archaeology is to reconstruct the lives of people in the past. The physical remains of the people themselves are key to this. From skeletons and bodies archaeologists are able to extract information ranging from what people ate to how long they lived and why they died. By combining careful study of skulls with a knowledge of the anatomy of faces it is even possible to re-create the faces of people who died hundreds or thousands of years ago.

The evidence

A wide variety of human remains are recovered by archaeologists. Occasionally, entire bodies are found, perhaps because they were mummified, frozen in ice, or buried in bogs. Such bodies hold a wealth of information. They reveal details like hair colour, tattoos and sometimes even fingerprints. More often, human remains are in the form of skeletons or individual bones. Occasionally, evidence survives even when the body and skeleton have completely disappeared. Burials at the early medieval site of Sutton Hoo in eastern England could only be recovered as outlines in the soil. The bodies had decayed completely, but they still left tell-tale chemical traces in the sandy soil.

One of the Sutton Hoo sand-bodies. The actual body has disappeared, but it has left its shape as a stain in the sandy soil.

A 19th-century archaeologist called Guiseppe Fiorelli made complete casts of some of the people killed in the eruption of Mount Vesuvius in AD 79, even though their bodies had long since disappeared. He did this by pouring plaster into the holes left in the hardened volcanic ash as the bodies decayed.

The final agonies of a man from Pompeii. His body was buried by falling ash from the volcano.

Part of a spine showing damage caused by osteo-arthritis. This is likely to belong to an older person.

What were they like?

Human skeletons and bone remains can provide valuable information about appearance, age at death, sex and even family relationships. Male bones are usually larger than female ones, giving an indication of sex. The way teeth have been worn down can give an approximate idea of age, as can the state of a skeleton's bone joints. Height can be estimated even from individual leg bones. And members of the same family can be identified from the shapes of their skulls and from their blood group (which is also discovered from an analysis of their bones).

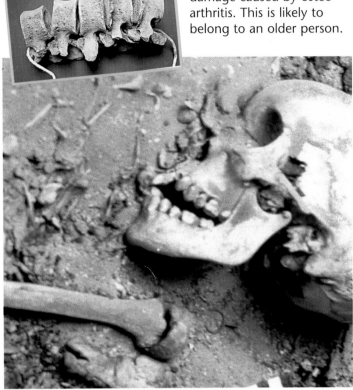

The skull and arm-bone (humerus) of a young person. Experts can see this is an adolescent because of the gap in the upper arm bone at the shoulder joint.

In focus RECONSTRUCTING FACES

The face of Seianti was built up around pegs fixed to a cast of her skull.

This is a reconstruction of the head of Seianti Hanunia Tlesnasa, an Italian noblewoman who died more than 2,000 years ago. By combining clues from the shape of her skull with a knowledge of how muscles, flesh and skin make up the face, scientists were able to build an accurate model to show what Seianti looked like. Similar models have been made of Philip of Macedon (the father of Alexander the Great) and of a man who died in the Alps more than 4,000 years ago.

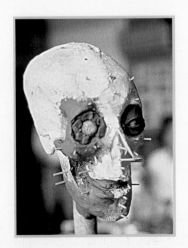

Life and death

Evidence from human remains can provide a wide variety of information about how people in the past lived and why they died. Teeth can indicate what sort of food was eaten. Deformities in bones may show what sort of work people did. Bones and flesh sometimes carry evidence of disease or violence. The amount of information that can be extracted from human remains has increased enormously in recent years with the development of new scientific techniques.

Looking inside bodies

Modern scientific techniques allow us to look inside bodies without damaging them. X-rays, and a similar technique called xeroradiography, allow archaeologists to see inside coffins or under the wrappings of a mummy. A body's internal organs can be viewed with the help of a 'CAT' scanner (normally used by doctors). The inside of a body can also be examined with a fibre-optic endoscope, which is a narrow flexible tube with a tiny camera fitted at its tip. Such techniques may provide surprising information. For example, an endoscope showed that the nose of the mummified pharaoh Rameses II had been packed with seeds and an animal bone so that the mummy bandages would not flatten it.

An Egyptian mummy is carefully placed in a CT scanner.

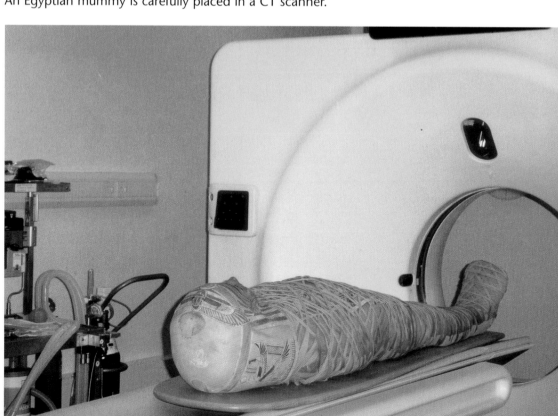

A CAT scan of the mummy of a child from ancient Egypt. You can see the bones inside the shape of the coffin. (The dots on his forehead are actually gold decorations on the coffin.)

Disease, deformity and death

Archaeologists use modern scientific techniques to tell them about illnesses people in the past suffered from and how they died. Where human flesh survives, it may contain parasites or evidence of viruses. Bones sometimes carry traces of diseases such as cancer. More often, they have evidence of fractures, breaks and other violent damage. A number of defects in the skeleton of Seianti (page 27) suggest that she was severely injured in adolescence. Her bones also indicate that this might have happened in a horse-riding accident, and that as she got older she suffered from arthritis and put on weight. Occasionally the cause of death is very obvious – the skeleton of an ancient Briton at the Iron Age hillfort of Maiden Castle, in southern England, had a large crossbow bolt in its spine!

The sarcophagus of Seianti. A horseriding accident early in her life may have caused her to put on weight as she grew older.

You can see the crossbow bolt that killed this man still stuck in his spine.

Profile — LINDOW MAN

'Lindow Man' is a body found in a bog in north-west England. Lindow Man lived about 2,000 years ago. He wore no clothing apart from an armband of fox fur, but he had painted skin. His fingernails were also manicured, and this suggests that he did not do any rough or heavy work. Analysis of his stomach contents even told scientists that his last meal was a cake of cereal. Lindow Man came to an unfortunate end. His skull had been smashed, his neck broken and his throat cut! He was then dropped face down into a pool in a bog. Perhaps he was killed as a sacrifice to the gods, or perhaps he was an executed criminal.

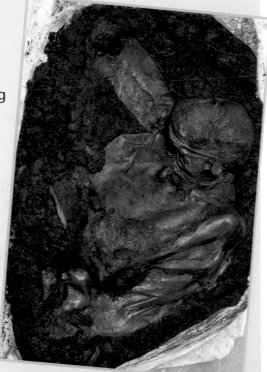

The future

The study of human remains is changing quickly. As well as examining bodies, scientists now study DNA, the tiny building blocks from which all life is made. Much of the evidence for movements of populations around the world thousands of years ago comes from such work.

What did they eat?

The leftovers from people's meals are the most direct source of evidence about what they ate. Information also comes from human remains, written evidence and the tools once used for hunting and fishing. This evidence allows archaeologists to build up a picture of what people normally ate over a period of time. Such information indicates important changes, such as when people started growing crops and keeping animals.

Leftovers

Preparing and eating a meal creates a lot of rubbish – the remains of bones, shells from seafood or fruit stones and seeds. Leftovers such as this can be the best clue archaeologists have to what people in the past ate. Some types of food, such as oysters, produce a lot of waste. Others, and especially plants, are not normally preserved. Some of the most important food remains are so small that they are invisible to the naked eye. Tiny crystals called phytoliths often survive even when plants have rotted away. They can provide clues about how food was harvested and cooked.

A huge pile of oyster shells. Amazingly, all of these oysters would only have provided the same amount of food as a single deer.

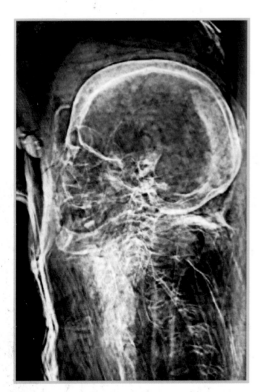

This CAT scan of an ancient Egyptian female mummy shows that the woman had only two teeth left when she died.

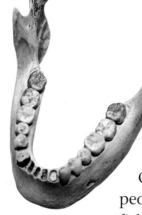

Teeth are often well preserved and may carry fascinating information about diet.

Human remains

Human remains often carry information about diet. Food leaves traces of chemicals in bones, and analysis of these can be very informative. One study showed that the diet of prehistoric people in Denmark changed from being mainly fish to mainly meat between the Mesolithic period and Bronze Age. Looking at the patterns different sorts of food make on human teeth can sometimes provide similar sorts of information. Occasionally, food is actually preserved inside human bodies, as in the case of Lindow Man (page 29) and some ancient Egyptian mummies.

Tools and containers

Tools and containers show what sorts of food have been eaten. Small hooks suggest that fish were caught, and sickles show that plants may have been harvested. The way tools have been used can sometimes be proved by studying the pattern of tiny scratches on their blades. Cutting meat and bone, for example, makes different scratches from cutting up plants. Scientists can also sometimes identify the remains of food from eating and drinking vessels, even if they are thousands of years old.

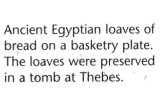

In ancient Greek and Roman times, large pots like this one were used to transport different sorts of food and drink. A pot of this shape is called an amphora.

Ancient Egyptian loaves of bread on a basketry plate. The loaves were preserved in a tomb at Thebes.

Archaeologists used to think these 12,500-year-old bone points from France were arrow tips or spikes for catching animals in traps. They now think the carefully-made bone tools are hooks for line fishing.

In focus — FARMING IN JORDAN

People have not always grown crops or kept animals for food. Farming first began in the near east around 9,000 - 10,000 BC and spread throughout Europe over the next 6000 years. It also developed independently in other areas of the world, including America and the far east. By about 8,000 BC, some people living in present Jordan and Israel began to depend chiefly on farming for their food, which allowed them to stay in one place all year round. As the result the population increased as farms began to develop.

Remains such as these burnt seeds from Tell es-Saïdeyeh in Jordan show that many early farmers grew cereals like wheat and barley.

Tools and technology

This stone tool from Olduvai Gorge in Africa is 1.8 million years old.

From the earliest axes of the Stone Age to the computers of the 21st century, people have used tools to change the world around them. The ability to make and use tools is what, in many people's eyes, makes humans different from other animals. In the 19th century, archaeologists began to divide up time by looking at changes in the tools people used. Names such as the Stone Age, Bronze Age and Iron Age are still used today. Modern archaeologists experiment with copies of ancient tools to see how effective they would have been. This is called experimental archaeology.

This glass fish was made in ancient Egypt, in the second millennium BC.

Fire

Fire is needed to make a wide variety of objects, from bronze knives to pottery bowls and glass windows. Learning to control fire has been one of humanity's most important technological advances. Fire was first used at least 1.5 million years ago. Baked-clay objects, including models of people and animals, were made in many places from about 30,000 years ago. Making glass and working metal both require very high temperatures. The first known glass vessels come from Egypt and were made only 3,500 years ago, in about 1500 BC.

Stone

The oldest man-made objects to survive are stone tools dating back more than two million years. At Olduvai Gorge, east Africa, archaeologists found stone chopping tools with the remains of some of the oldest early humans. Other tools – perhaps made of wood or bone – may have been used this long ago, but these have long since rotted away. Stone tools are sometimes hard to understand because no other evidence survives with them. Some archaeologists have tried to make stone tools themselves. Doing this gives them some idea of how the tools were made, what they were used for and how much time and effort was needed to create them.

An archaeologist with copies of stone tools.

What was it for?

There are a number of possible ways to discover the function of tools from the distant past. Some of these are scientific. Looking at the tiny scratches on the edges of stone tools sometimes gives clues about what they may have cut. Traces of blood on tools occasionally show which animals the tools were used to skin and cut up. Others methods are based on looking at how tools are used by present-day people such as Australian Aboriginals. And experimenting with modern copies of old tools is a good way of testing theories about what the implements might have been used for.

▲ There are at least 40 different theories about the function of this antler tool from prehistoric France. The most popular suggests that it was used to straighten arrows.

This wooden sickle was ▶ used to harvest corn in ancient Egypt. It is made in the shape of a cow's jawbone, with sharp flints where the teeth would be. Scientists can analyse the wear on the flints, and the traces of corn left on them, to find out what kind of crops the sickle was used to cut.

Industrial archaeology

Archaeologists do not just study the distant past. They also investigate some of the changes that have taken place in recent centuries. One of the biggest developments in the last 300 years has been in the way things are made. This change is called industrialization. Archaeologists excavating old industrial sites, such as factories and china works, can recover fascinating details of manufacturing processes that have fallen out of use and have been forgotten.

Ironbridge Gorge was the world's first cast-iron bridge. It was built in 1777-9 and it has become a symbol of the Industrial Revolution.

Trade and exchange

This ancient Greek pot was signed by the man who made it, Exekias. You can see his name behind the warrior's right arm (and in the inset picture). Archaeologists know that Exekias worked in Athens around 540–530 BC.

The study of trade and exchange between people in the past is an increasingly important part of archaeology. Trade often indicates an exchange of ideas as well as objects. The best evidence for trade is the movement of objects – finding something such as a pot far from where it was made, for example. Coins and some other objects tell us exactly where they were made, but for most objects, archaeologists have to work out where they came from, judging by their style and the material from which they are made.

Materials

The materials from which objects are made can tell archaeologists a lot about trade in the past. Materials, including stone, pottery and metal, often have distinctive 'signatures' that can be understood by scientists and show exactly where they came from. A stone axe head, for example, may be found hundreds of miles from the place in which the stone was quarried. This suggests that either the axe head or the stone itself was traded. Obsidian, or volcanic glass, was highly valued for making tools in the past. The study of obsidian tools in areas like the Near East and Central America shows that some were traded over distances of hundreds of kilometres.

A decorated obsidian blade from the Mayan city of Tikal (in modern Mexico). Obsidian was highly prized and traded over long distances.

How society works

Anthropologists are people who try to understand the past by studying the way people have behaved in more recent times. The work of anthropologists has helped archaeologists realize that goods may move around the world for reasons other than trade. In some societies, giving beautiful and valuable presents was a way of increasing your own importance. Objects as varied as Iron Age gold torcs, Chinese silk robes and Mexican turquoise mosaics may have been given as gifts rather than bought and sold.

Magnificent objects like this turquoise mosaic serpent from ancient Mexico were sometimes used as gifts.

In focus THE SILK ROAD

Goods are sometimes traded over distances of thousands of kilometres. One of the most extraordinary trade routes of the past was the 'Silk Road', which joined China and India to Rome, Greece and the Near East. Luxuries such as silk from China and spices from India were exchanged for gold, silver and other goods. A number of sites on the Silk Road were excavated by the archaeologist Sir Aurel Stein (1862–1943) in the early 20th century. He discovered a wealth of objects ranging from silk temple banners to such everyday goods as ancient wooden chopsticks.

◀ Thousands of Roman coins are found in India, where they were exchanged for luxuries like spices.

One of the silk paintings found by Stein at Dunhuang in China, one of the Silk Road sites. ▶

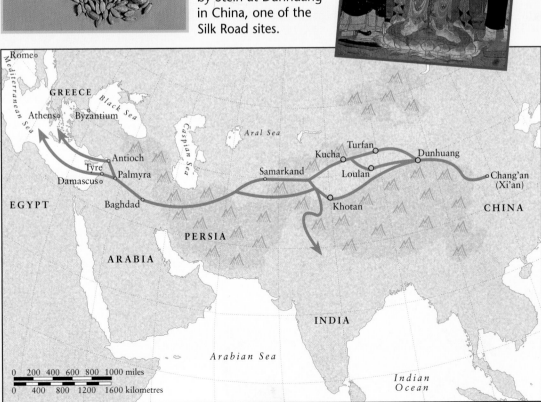

A map of the Silk Road, showing some of the most important sites excavated by Aurel Stein.

What did they think?

It is impossible to know what people who died hundreds or thousands of years ago thought, unless they wrote their ideas down. But the remains people left behind do give hints about why they behaved as they did. Understanding and explaining the past is the great challenge facing modern archaeology. One thing that makes humans very different from other species is their ability to use symbols. Symbols are pictures, words or objects that represent thoughts.

Ritual and belief

We will never be able to understand fully the beliefs of past people who have left no written records. However, archaeologists do sometimes find what seems to be evidence of beliefs. It is reasonable, for example, to suggest that Iron Age people in parts of Europe believed that some places were sacred. Objects, including gold objects, bodies, and deliberately broken weapons and shields, were thrown into certain rivers and marshes.

This Iron Age shield was found in the River Thames.

Burial

One source of evidence about what people in the past thought and believed comes from how they buried their dead. The fact that people were buried at all suggests respect for the dead person, and perhaps a belief in an afterlife. Definite evidence of deliberate burial is known from more than 20,000 years ago. At Arene Candide in Italy, for example, archaeologists excavated more than 20 individuals. Some were at least 20,500 years old and several were buried with grave goods, including ornaments of sea shells and bone.

The grave of the 'young prince' from Arene Candide. He was about 12 years old, and wore a cap of sea shells.

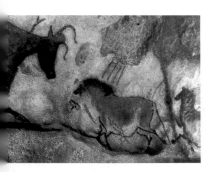

Pictures

Pictures help us to understand how people in the past thought about the world. The earliest known pictures come from Ice Age caves, such as the ones at Lascaux in France. Here, paintings of horses, aurochs (wild cattle) and other animals show the importance of these animals to the people who used the caves more than 17,000 years ago.

Writing

The appearance of writing shows a new stage of development. Writing is a very effective way of communicating and describing the world. The earliest known form of writing is called cuneiform. It developed in Mesopotamia (modern Iraq) more than 5,000 years ago. Egyptian hieroglyphs are also known from about 5,000 years ago. Most early writing tells us about official matters – perhaps the achievements of a king. But in societies such as ancient Greece, where many people could read and write, we also learn about the lives of ordinary men and women.

This cuneiform tablet was written between 2,350 and 2,250 BC. It records payments of barley to 200 workmen.

Egyptian hieroglyphs from a papyrus scroll of spells and prayers called the Book of the Dead. This papyrus belonged to a man called Panedjem (about 990-960 BC).

This Greek coin is about 2,500 years old. The words on it read 'I am the badge of Phanes'. This suggests that many people who used coins like this could read.

Profile   CHAMPOLLION (1790–1832)

For many centuries visitors to Egypt were puzzled by the strange picture writing that they found on monuments and tombs. In 1799 a slab of dark stone was found near Rosetta (modern Rashid). The 'Rosetta Stone' became famous because in 1822 it enabled a young Frenchman, Jean François Champollion, to unravel the mystery of hieroglyphic writing. There was an inscription on the stone, carved in three different sorts of writing – hieroglyphic, demotic (another sort of Egyptian script) and Greek. The Greek language was already known and so Champollion was able to discover how the two Egyptian scripts worked. After this discovery many hieroglyphic inscriptions could be read and much was found out about the life and customs of the ancient Egyptians.

This slab of Egyptian stone carries a king's decree written in Greek and in an Egyptian script called demotic, as well as in hieroglyphs. Comparison of the three allowed Champollion to decipher hieroglyphs for the first time.

The future of archaeology

rchaeology is becoming increasingly successful in understanding the past. New technology and new methods are allowing us to expand and update our knowledge all the time. But archaeology is also facing new challenges. The remains of our past are being destroyed more quickly than we can hope to study them. And new issues are being raised about who the past actually belongs to.

Who owns the past?

Millions of objects from the past are in museums and private collections around the world. But who really owns them? The people who have them now or the descendants of the people they once belonged to? A number of museums have returned the bones of people, such as Australian Aboriginals or New Zealand Maoris, to their modern descendants. Some governments are now demanding that museums or individuals return many other objects that were taken from their countries in the past. But the question of ownership is not an easy one.

The head of the Egyptian queen Nefertiti in Berlin and a frieze from the Parthenon sculptures in The British Museum. Should they be returned to Egypt and Greece?

Archaeology and the public

Archaeologists have a duty to share their knowledge with the public. They do this in part by publishing reports on excavations and discoveries. More and more archaeologists are also spending time with the public, giving talks in schools or tours of excavations. This work is vital to the future of archaeology, since, directly or indirectly, the public pays for archaeological work to take place.

Schoolchildren study Roman coins.

Worldwide conservation

Today we are more aware than ever of the need to preserve the past. At the same time, more sites are being destroyed every year due to increases in building, agriculture and pollution. In Japan, for example, more than 6,000 sites were destroyed in 1980 alone. Most excavations occur when archaeologists are called in just before a new motorway or building is being constructed, and they have to recover as much information as they can in as short a time as possible.

Please don't touch! Visitors are kept at a distance from the world-famous monument of Stonehenge in England to protect its ancient stones.

The success of archaeology is itself a problem. Millions of people visit archaeological sites every year and the sheer number of visitors can actually damage some sites. Visitors are now prevented from touching the standing stones at Stonehenge in southern England because of the damage done to the monument in the past. New laws are helping some of these problems, but more still needs to be done if we are to preserve our past.

Scientific advances are changing our understanding of the past. This apparatus uses an argon plasma, heated to around 10,000 degrees Celsius, to measure accurately the different elements in a sample of metal.

Archaeology and technology

Archaeology has been transformed by modern technological changes. Archaeologists can now accurately date many types of object. They can analyse objects made from metal, stone or pottery to tell where the raw materials came from and how they were made. And they can use computers to reconstruct long-vanished buildings or even to test the methods used to build monuments. Technology continues to advance, and it is certain that the 21st century will see many developments that transform our understanding of the past.

The fog clears

Only 200 years ago a Danish scholar called Rasmus Nyerup (1759–1829) wrote that we knew so little about the time before the Greeks and Romans that it was 'wrapped in a thick fog'. Today, that fog has cleared a little, and our understanding of even the distant past is increasing. But there is still much we don't know. In many cases we know reasonably well what people in the past did but have little understanding of why they did it. Explaining, as well as describing, human behaviour has become the focus for archaeology in the 21st century.

Further reading

For children

Harris, G. and Pemberton, D. *The British Museum Encyclopaedia of Ancient Egypt*. London: British Museum Press, 1999.

McIntosh, J. *Archaeology, Eyewitness Guides*. London: Dorling Kindersley, 2000.

Pemberton, D. *Egyptian Mummies – People from the Past*. London: British Museum Press, 2000.

Orna-Ornstein, J. *The Story of Money*. London: British Museum Press, 1997.

For adults

Barker, P. *Techniques of Archaeological Excavation*. 3rd edn. London: Batsford, 1993.

Greene, K. *Archaeology – An Introduction: The History, Principles and Methods of Modern Archaeology*. 3rd edn. London: Routledge, 1996.

McIntosh, J. *The Practical Archaeologist: How we know what we know about the past*. London: Thames and Hudson, 1999.

Renfrew, C. and Bahn, P. *Archaeology: Theories, Methods and Practice*. 2nd edn. London: Thames and Hudson, 1996.

Scarre, C., ed. *Past Worlds: The Times Atlas of Archaeology*. New York: Random House Value Publishing, 1995.

Index